Animal Look-Alikes

Butterflies and Moths

Joanne Mattern

RED CHAIR •PRESS•

Animal Look-Alikes is produced and published by Red Chair Press:

Red Chair Press LLC   PO Box 333   South Egremont, MA 01258-0333

www.redchairpress.com

About the Author

Joanne Mattern is the author of nearly 350 books for children and teens. She began writing when she was a little girl and just never stopped! Joanne loves nonfiction because she enjoys bringing science topics to life and showing young readers that nonfiction is full of compelling stories! Joanne lives in the Hudson Valley of New York State with her husband, four children, and several pets, which look nothing alike!

Publisher's Cataloging-In-Publication Data
Names: Mattern, Joanne, 1963-
Title: Butterflies and moths / Joanne Mattern.

Description: [South Egremont, Massachusetts] : Red Chair Press, [2018] | Series: Animal look-alikes | Interest age level: 006-010. | Includes science vocabulary, fun facts, and trivia about each type of animal. | "Core content library." | Includes bibliographical references. | Summary: "Colorful or dull. Wings up or wings down. Active at night or prefers daylight. Is it a butterfly or a moth? Look inside to learn how these beautiful insects are alike and how they differ."-- Provided by publisher.

Identifiers: LCCN 2016947283 | ISBN 978-1-63440-210-1 (library hardcover) | ISBN 978-1-63440-215-6 (ebook)

Subjects: LCSH: Butterflies--Juvenile literature. | Moths--Juvenile literature. | CYAC: Butterflies. | Moths.

Classification: LCC QL544.2 .M38 2018 (print) | LCC QL544.2 (ebook) | DDC 595.78--dc23

Illustrations by Tim Haggerty.

Photo credits: Shutterstock except for the following: p. 17: Ingimage.

Printed in Canada

102017 1P FRNS18

Table of Contents

Butterfly or Moth?

You see a flash of wings in the sky. Is the creature you see a butterfly or a moth? Sometimes it is hard to tell. These two animals have a lot in common. But even though some things about them are the same, there are also many ways to tell which animal is which. Let's take a closer look at butterflies and moths!

Diadem
butterfly

Luna moth

Amazing Insects

Butterflies and moths are both members of the insect family. There are more insects on Earth than any another species of animal. Insects have many special features.

One of the most important things about insects is that their bodies are made up of three parts. These parts are the **abdomen**, the **thorax**, and the head. Insects also have their skeletons on the outside of their bodies instead of the inside! An insect's skeleton is a hard shell that protects the soft organs inside. With butterflies and moths, the wings hold the skeleton.

Butterflies and moths are part of an order of insects called Lepidoptera. This is a Greek word meaning "scale wing". There are 120 different families of moths, but only six different families of butterflies.

Now You Know!

There are about 250,000 different species of Lepidoptera, but only about 20,000 of them are butterflies.

Purple-edged copper butterfly

Head

Thorax

Abdomen

Frenulum

On the Wing

All insects have six legs. Insects also have wings. Some insects have very tiny wings. But when you look at a butterfly or moth, it is easy to see their wings.

Both butterflies and moths have four wings. A butterfly's wings are not connected to each other, but a moth's wings are connected. A moth has a special body part called the frenulum. The frenulum hooks the rear wing to the front wing on each side of the moth's body. Because the wings are connected, they move together when the moth flies. Butterflies do not have a frenulum.

Now You Know!

Many animals like to eat butterflies and moths, including birds, bats, frogs, skunks, mice, spiders, and wasps.

The wings are an important way to tell butterflies and moths apart. Butterfly wings are usually large and colorful. A moth's wings are usually smaller and not as bright. Many moths have gray, brown, or white wings. These dull colors work as **camouflage** to help the moth hide from **predators**.

Some butterflies have bright circles on their wings. These circles look like giant eyes. A butterfly can show these spots to scare predators away.

Butterflies and moths also hold their wings differently when they are not flying. A butterfly holds its wings straight up and down over its back. A moth holds its wings down to cover its body or spreads them out to the sides.

Tiny scales cover the wings and bodies of both moths and butterflies. These scales are actually a kind of hair. Some moths even look furry, while butterflies look smooth.

Brown moths disappear on tree bark.

Antennae at Work

Another body part that all insects have are antennae. A butterfly has thin, straight antennae. A butterfly antenna looks like a stick with a round club at the end. A moth's antennae look very different. Moth antennae are usually thicker than a butterfly's. A moth's antennae sometimes looks like a feather.

Antennae help both moths and butterflies to find their way around. These **organs** help them sense when food is nearby. Antennae also help butterflies and moths sense light and darkness. And they help males and females find each other when it is time to mate.

Power Word: Antennae is the proper plural form of antenna. It comes from the word for the long 'yard arm' on a ship's mast.

13

Warm Homes

Butterflies and moths live all over the world, but moths live in more places than butterflies do. Moths are found on every continent except Antarctica. They are found in forests, woods, grasslands, and even in the desert.

Now You Know!

Every year, monarch butterflies migrate from the northern parts of the United States and Canada to Mexico. They migrate to the same places every year. Scientists are still not sure how the monarchs find their way.

Because they are insects, butterflies and moths are cold-blooded. That means they cannot control their body temperature. If the weather gets too cold, the insect will freeze to death. For this reason, many butterflies and moths live in tropical places. Some butterflies **migrate** to warmer places when the weather gets cold.

Owl butterfly on a spiky cactus

Day and Night

Another way to tell butterflies and moths apart is the time of day when you see them. Most butterflies are **diurnal**. That means they are active during the day. Most moths are **nocturnal**. They are active at night.

Many kinds of moths are attracted to bright lights. You will often see moths gathered around a porch light or flying around the bright lights at a ball field or stadium. Butterflies do not do this.

Now You Know!

Moths and butterflies do not live very long. A moth usually lives from two to eleven months. A butterfly also lives less than one year.

A Big Change

One of the most important things butterflies and moths have in common is that both go through a **metamorphosis**. That means their bodies change completely as they grow.

The life cycle of a butterfly or moth has four stages. Both butterflies and moths hatch from eggs. These eggs are laid on plants that the creature likes to eat. This means that as soon as the insect hatches, it has food to eat right away. Some moths lay about 40 eggs, while others lay up to 1,000. Some butterflies also lay up to 100 eggs. Since most eggs are eaten by predators, it is important for these insects to lay so many eggs.

Now You Know!

A butterfly's eggs can be as small as the head of a pin!

Wasps have been known to eat butterfly eggs.

Tawny coster butterfly laying eggs

19

Newly hatched gypsy moth caterpillars

Swallowtail butterfly caterpillar with molted skin

When the eggs hatch, the creature that comes out does not look anything like a butterfly or moth. Instead, it is a caterpillar. Caterpillars do not have wings. Their bodies can be long and colorful. A caterpillar has strong jaws.

The caterpillar chews its way out of the egg. As soon as it hatches, it starts to eat the plants around it. A caterpillar's only job is to eat. The more it eats, the bigger it grows. As the caterpillar grows, its skin gets too tight. Finally, the skin splits apart, and the caterpillar crawls out with a new covering. This process is called molting. A caterpillar can molt four or five times during its life.

Now You Know!

Caterpillars can do a lot of damage to trees as they eat.

Moth cocoon

Cocoon or Chrysalis?

After two to four weeks, the caterpillar stops eating. It finds a safe place, such as a branch to hang from, or a hole in the ground. Then it sheds its skin for the last time.

Moth caterpillars produce long threads of silk. The caterpillar spins the silk around its body to create a case called a cocoon. The silk threads get hard when air touches them to make a strong case that protects the creature inside.

A butterfly caterpillar does not spin a cocoon. Instead, it covers itself with a hard skin called a chrysalis. A chrysalis is harder and stronger than a cocoon. Inside both a cocoon and a chrysalis, amazing changes are happening.

DO
NOT
DISTURB

Inside the cocoon or chrysalis, the caterpillar's body changes into a liquid. All its body parts disappear. Then the creature's body reforms into a moth or a butterfly. This is the final stage of metamorphosis.

Metamorphosis can take a few weeks or a few months. Finally, the adult creature cracks open its cocoon or chrysalis. When the moth or butterfly comes out, it is wet and cannot fly. It sits for a few minutes, flapping its wings to dry off. Finally, the new creature flies away. Its life-changing metamorphosis is complete.

The word "metamorphosis" comes from the Greek words for "shape changing."

A swallowtail butterfly emerges from its chrysalis.

25

Blue tIger butterfly

New Foods

Caterpillars chew on leaves, but butterflies and moths eat different foods. During metamorphosis, a caterpillar's jaws change into an organ called a proboscis. A proboscis is a long, thin tube that can curl up to stay out of the way. This proboscis can't chew food the way a caterpillar's jaws can. Instead, the butterfly or moth uses it to suck a sweet liquid called **nectar** out of flowers.

A butterfly or moth's antennae help it find flowers that have nectar the insect likes. Once it finds a tasty plant, the creature sits on the edge of the flower or flies in front of it. Then it unrolls its long proboscis and sucks up the nectar, just like you drink juice through a straw.

Proboscis

Saving Butterflies and Moths

It may seem like butterflies and moths are everywhere, but many of these insects are **endangered**. Many butterflies and moths lose their homes when their **habitats** are destroyed. Cutting down trees or grasslands takes away the places these insects live and the plants they eat. Pollution and **pesticides** can also kill butterflies and moths.

Many people are trying to save endangered butterflies and moths. Organizations protect their habitats or set up new habitats where these insects can live. You and your friends and family can help too by planting gardens with plants that butterflies and moths like to eat.

The Queen Alexandra's birdwing is the largest butterfly in the world. Its wingspan measures up to 12 inches (30.5 cm) across. It is also the rarest butterfly because most of the rain forests where it lives have been cut down.

Beautiful Flight

Butterflies and moths are not the same. Many things about their bodies and their lives are different. However, many things

are also the same. Both butterflies and moths are beautiful creatures that have a special place in our world. The features that help us tell them apart make each species unique and wonderful.

A butterfly house in Ecuador

This scarlet mormon butterfly emerged from its chrysalis in a butterfly museum.

Glossary

abdomen the back part of an insect's body

camouflage coloring or markings on an animal's skin that help it blend in with its surroundings

diurnal active during the day

endangered in danger of dying out

habitats places where animals and plants live

metamorphosis in an insect, the process of changing from one body stage to another

migrate to travel from one place to another, often during different seasons

nectar a sweet liquid found in some flowers

nocturnal active during the night

organs parts of the body that have a specific function

pesticides poison that kills insects

predators animals that hunt other animals for food

thorax the middle part of an insect's body

Read More in the Library

Marsh, Laura. *Butterflies* (Great Migrations). National Geographic Kids, 2010.

Simon, Seymour. *Butterflies*. Harper Collins, 2011.